THIS IS A STORY.

DR. KIM D. HARRIS

THESE WORDS ARE FOR YOU & ME & US & WE

each one teach one.

This is a story about
FOUR
BLACK PEOPLE

EVERYBODY
BLACK

SOMEBODY
BLACK

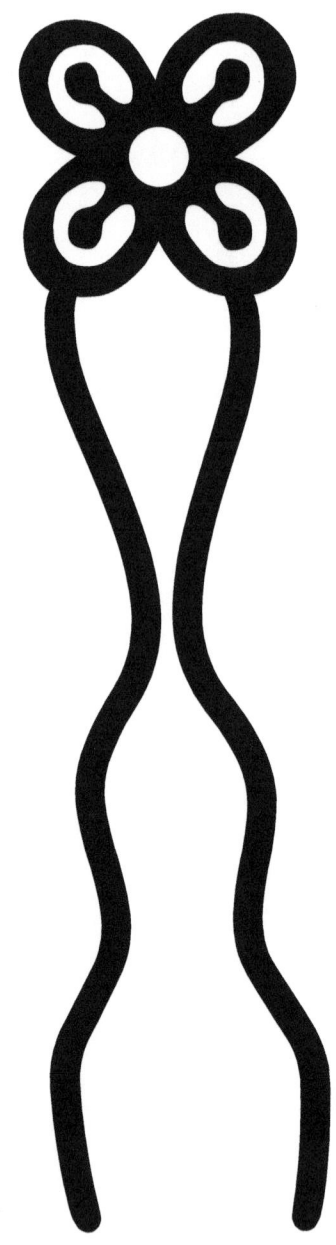

ANYBODY

BLACK

and...

NOBODY
BLACK

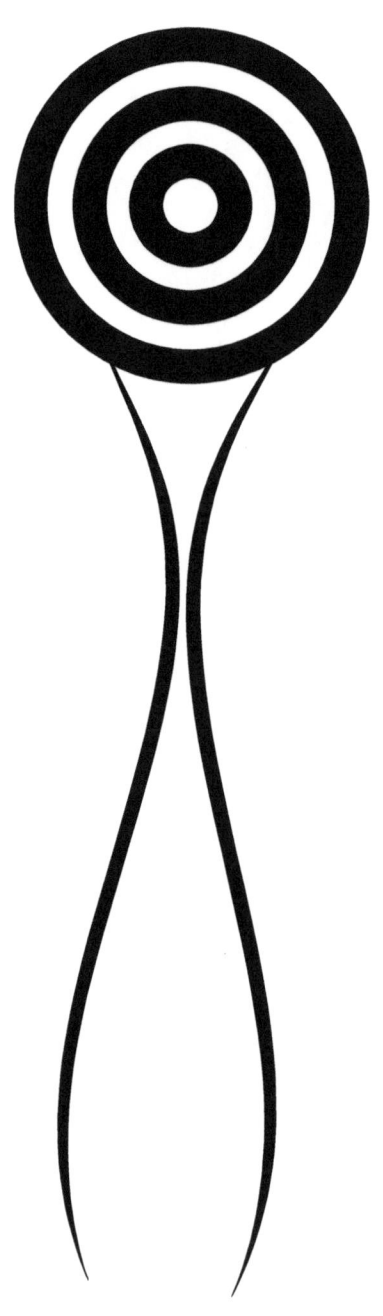

You see there was an important job to be

DONE

A job that requires

LIVING & LOVING

each other

and

working together as

ONE

EVERYBODY
BLACK

Thought
THAT...

SOMEBODY
BLACK

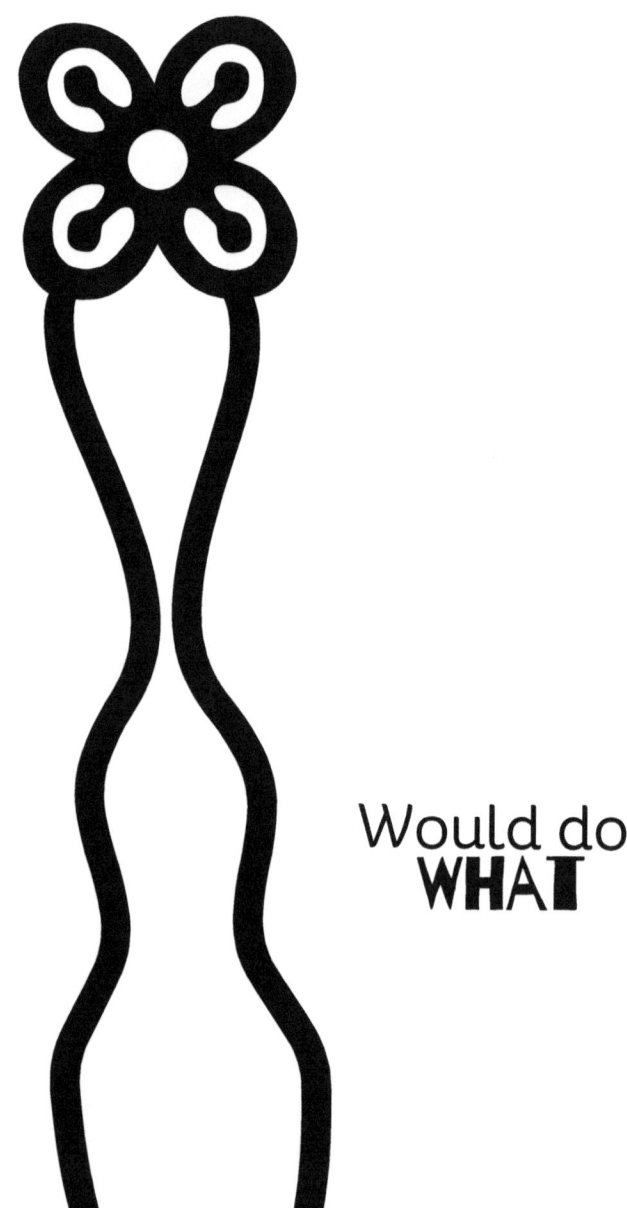

Would do
WHAT

ANYBODY
BLACK

Could have
DONE

But...
NOBODY
BLACK

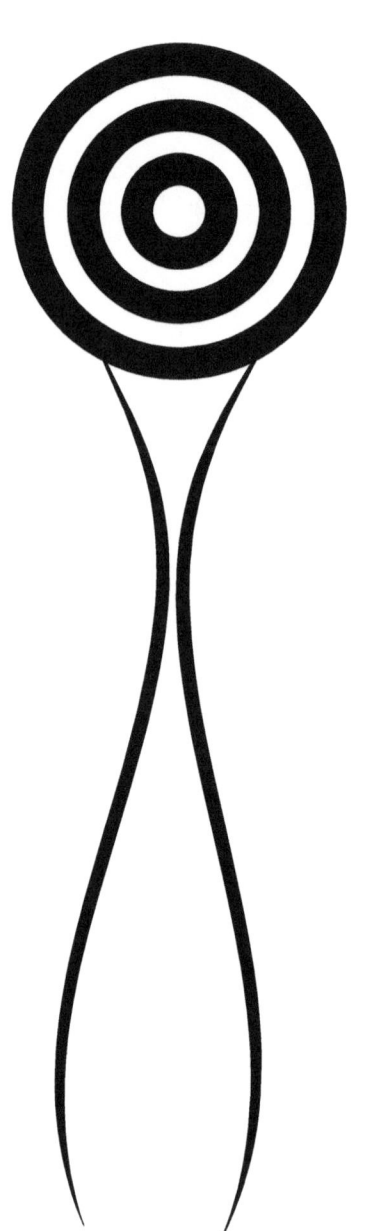

Did
IT...

SOMEBODY
BLACK

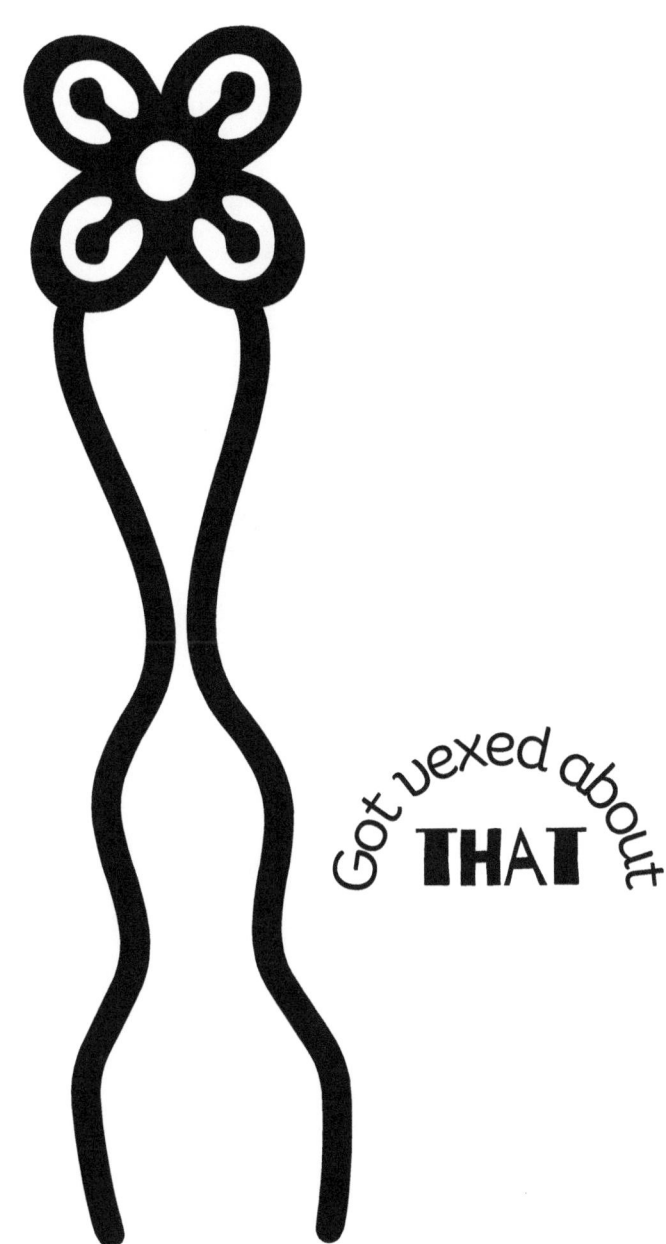

Got vexed about THAT

So they decided to meet with each

OTHER

They reflected deeply on the question

IF NOT, NOW WHEN?

They decided that it is now or **NEVER**

To be like birds of a feather flocked

TOGETHER

In any kind of WEATHER

So they went to the four corners of the EARTH

SPREADING THEIR MESSAGE

about

peace, love **HARMONY** and

CULTURAL SUSTAINABILITY

They planted seeds in other black folks to

UNITE

To teach their children about their **CULTU**RE

BLACK HISTORY IS WORLD HISTORY

and their

HERITAGE

To learn to grow their own

FOOD

So they can eat and

feed those in their

NEIGHBORHOOD

To **BUILD** and To **CREATE**

Everything they need to **SU**RVIVE & **TH**RIVE

so that they can **RISE** as a **POWERFUL PEOPLE**

and always
REMEMBER

that POWERFUL PEOPLE do POWERFUL things

and that in **UNITY** there is

STRENGTH

which is the key to building their

LEGACy

for their future generations to seeee e

ADINKRA MEANINGS

 A symbol for authority, leadership, and charisma. Also a symbol for the circle of life. Known as Adinkrahene.

 Wooden comb. A symbol of feminine consideration or good feminine qualities such as patience, prudence, fondness, love, and care.. Known as Duafe.

 Sack of cola nuts. A symbol for affllence, abudance, and unity. Known as Besa Saka..

 Conjoined crocodiles. A symbol of unity in diversity giving a common destiny.. Known as Dwenkyemfunefu.

 A symbol of the wisdom of learning from the past to build for the future.. Known as Sankofa.

 A rams head. A symbol of humilty and strength with a sense of balance. Known as Dwennimmem.

 A symbol expressing the omnipotence of God. Known as Gye Nyame.

 A symbol of the heart acknowledging the spiirt of patience and tolerance. Known as Akoma.

About The Author

Dr. Kim D. Harris

I am an advocate for creativity that promotes cultural sustainability and heritage preservation.

You see, I believe that it is important to reflect deeply with our children about the resilience that is in each and everyone of us. It is important to show them that they are loved, supported, and powerful.

www.ingramcontent.com/pod-product-compliance
Lightning Source LLC
Chambersburg PA
CBHW041526120626
46551CB00018B/2594